From the Author:

In February of 2019, I wanted to make some changes in my life. I realized that I had failed to love me authentically. I decided I wanted to learn to love me. I also wanted to share my journey to self-love with others in hopes that the changes I've made would encourage others in their journey to self-love. I wanted to change the way I love me and the way I treat me.

Statistically it takes 21 days to create or break a habit. I wanted to break the habit of self-neglect and create a habit of self-love. For 21 days I committed to posting a self-love declaration for 21 days on social media. In doing so it was my effort to engage others in their journey. During the 21 days of posting several people said the post helped them and the information would make a great book. They felt the information should to be shared with the world and from that the writing of this workbook journal began.

I completed the 21 days of posting and in the process, I recommitted to loving me. I am committed of no longer neglecting me. I made several promises to myself throughout the journey to self-love and my desire is by the end of this workbook, you would have done the same. Take the time to do the work so that you can be a better version of you.

In this workbook you will find 21 self-love lessons to guide you to your desired end result of learning you and getting to know the true you.

Each day there is a self-love lesson, a self-love exercise, and a self-love journal exercise. There are journal pages in the back of the book for you to complete your exercises.

Embrace each day as a new opportunity to change the narrative and LOVE YOU.

About the Author

Hello, my name is Mechelle D. Canady and I'm a seasoned Event Planner, Master Certified Life Coach, and Innovator who is driven by an unwavering entrepreneurial spirit. My dedication to helping people become their best versions has also earned me the reputation as "Mrs. GetU2Gether."

Throughout the past decade or so, I have gained extensive experience in multiple industries, including event planning (since 2004), business consulting (since 2009), and Professional Christian Life Coach (since 2017). Master Life Coach and Certified Trainer (2019) and I have launched Embrace You Training Solutions and we Certify Life Coaches and Trainers. I published my first book in November 2017 titled Frozen 3A's My Journey to True Forgiveness. Since then I have co-authored 3 more books. Helping others is my passion and now I am able to help other authors publish their books independently with my new publishing copy C-Sharp Publishing.

As a passionate Change Agent, I am on a mission to **Impact**, **Impart**, and, **Empower** as many people as possible, and ultimately create positive change that will continue transforming lives for future generations. I deeply believe that each and every one of us possesses infinite potential, and when we harness that potential, the possibilities are truly endless.

In addition to pursuing my Bachelor's degree in Supervision & Management, I currently serve as the Founder & Operator of The Next Chapter 4 Me Consulting Planning & More, the CEO of Coach Mechelle Canady Ministries, Founder of Prissy Printing, the Head Baker of Tyler Tasty Treats and the Co-Founder of #iGrow a personal growth and development company. I sit on the Board of Directors for Players by The Sea, a non-profit community theater.

I am currently working on a workbook titled "Me vs. Me: The Inner me is the Enemy". Due to be released this year. My heart desire is to leave a legacy that impacts generations to come by being a World Changer.

I AM COMPLETELY IN LOVE with ME

Day 1 Learn Your Love Language

Love is a language spoken by everyone. But we often have difficulty communicating our love to those we are in a relationship. Most of us don't know what we need from those we are in relationship because we are unknowing of what we need for ourselves.

In this journey to self-love I think there is no better place to start than with learning your love language. By learning your love language, you will be able to better identify how to speak or communicate love to others and how to receive love from others.

What we love, we should protect and treat with high esteem. We do things to make sure we preserve the thing we love because we love it. Those things we love less we value less. We take less care; we don't always protect it and we will give it way easily. The same thing goes for ourselves. When you love yourself and value yourself, you will protect yourself, treat yourself with love and hold yourself at high esteem. But when you don't love yourself you will allow others to use and abuse you, disrespect you and disregard your value.

You may not have learned to love yourself as a child or you may have found yourself in a low place. It's not too late for to start today. So, on this journey to self-love, learning the language of love will lead you through the rest of the journey.

In order to be better in relationship with others we must first master relationship with ourselves.

Gary Chapman in his book "The 5 Love Languages" he has identified 5 ways we love and receive love.

1. Words of Affirmations
2. Physical Touch
3. Receiving Gifts
4. Quality Time
5. Act of Service

Self-Love Exercise: Read the definitions below and determine your primary and secondary love language. Write down your love languages on your journal pages. Read the how to communicate section and think about ways you can better communicate to yourself using your love languages. Today take action by using the suggested action that corresponds with your primary and secondary love language. Then journal your commitment to speaking love and acting in love.

Self-Love Journal Exercise: Write your thoughts on your new discover of your love language. With discovering the way, you give and receive love will allow you the ability to communicate to yourself and others the type of love you need going forth.

WHICH LOVE LANGUAGE?	HOW TO COMMUNICATE	ACTIONS TO TAKE
WORDS OF AFFIRMATION	Encourage, affirm, appreciate, empathize. Listen actively.	Send an unexpected note, text, or card. Encourage genuinely and often.
PHYSICAL TOUCH	Non-verbal - use body language and touch to emphasize love.	Hug, kiss, hold hands, show physical affection regularly. Make intimacy a thoughtful priority.
RECEIVING GIFTS	Thoughtfulness, make your spouse a priority, speak purposefully.	Give thoughtful gifts and gestures. Small things matter in a big way. Express gratitude when receiving a gift.
QUALITY TIME	Uninterrupted and focused conversations. One-on-one time is critical.	Create special moments together, take walks and do small things with your spouse. Weekend getaways are huge.
ACTS OF SERVICE	Use action phrases like "I'll help...". They want to know you're with them, partnered with them.	Do chores together or make them breakfast in bed. Go out of your way to help alleviate their daily workload.

GRAPHIC BY FIERCEMARRIAGE.COM
BASED ON "*THE 5 LOVE LANGUAGES*", A BOOK BY DR. GARY CHAPMAN

Tell Yourself Daily

YOU ALONE ARE ENOUGH
YOU HAVE NOTHING TO
PROVE TO ANYONE

— Maya Angelou

Day 2 I AM ENOUGH

One day I was at work talking with my good friend Taylor. As we were talking, she was sharing her journey to receiving her Master's Degree and one of her professors was teaching about the "Imposter Syndrome. She was sharing with me the information and the book they were reading on the Imposter Syndrome and it really hit home. She described the feeling I felt after every great moment in my life. I had never even heard of such a syndrome so I wanted to know more about it.

The definition of the Imposter Syndrome is a psychological pattern in which an individual doubt their accomplishments and has a persistent internalized fear of being exposed as a fraud. I looked it up because I have experienced this feeling many times. I found myself at my lowest when I should have been at my highest because of a great accomplishment. I needed to understand why in my success I felt like an imposter.

I bought two of the books Taylor recommended Impostor Syndrome (The Arcadia Project) by Mishell Baker and Lean In Women, Work, and the Will to Lead by Sheryl Sandberg, and those books assisted and empowered me to learn how to stand in my success because I AM ENOUGH!!

Often my inner critic made me feel unworthy to be celebrated. I felt I wasn't enough. But after reading and soul searching, I decided to start to affirming myself and whenever my inner critic tells me I'm not worthy, I would boldly tell myself I AM ENOUGH. If I can work hard and put the time and effort needed to accomplish my goal. I'm worthy of the victory.

I wrote it on a sticky note and put it on my mirror to remind myself that I AM ENOUGH. Daily as I go to the bathroom and look at myself in the mirror and that sticky note is a constant reminder that I am victorious and worthy of every success I achieve and so are you.

Don't allow the voices in your head to make you feel less than enough. You are fearfully and wondrously made. You have the ability to be everything you have been placed on this earth to be. YOU ARE ENOUGH.

Self-Love Exercise: Write on the sticky note I AM ENOUGH. Place it somewhere that you will see it daily. As often as you pass by it, read it out loud to yourself.

Self-Love Journal Exercise: Write about a time when you felt like a failure in your success. Write your thoughts your feeling and what made you feel like you were an imposter. It is important to first identify the behavior in order to fix it. So, the next time you are feeling unworthy love yourself enough to say out loud I AM ENOUGH!!!!

Day 3 Compliment Yourself

I was talking with my daughter Victoria in the car on the way to church one Sunday. I was complimenting her on how beautiful she looked and she said "Ma I don't really know how to take compliments from people." That made me think back to the time when I didn't know how to take compliments from people either. Whenever people would compliment me, I would always make what I call a "counter-compliment." For example, I'm a true bargain shopper so I look great most times at an unbelievable price. The moment someone says "you look super cute" my counter-compliment is "I only paid 20.00 for this outfit". My counter-compliment totally discounted the compliment and devalued the compliment. Think about your response to when people compliment you. Does it make you feel uncomfortable, do you counter-compliment, or do you simply say thank you?

I discovered that I wasn't able to accept compliments from others because I never complimented myself. The lack of love for myself made we feel unworthy to be complimented so I cancelled it out with a statement to devalue whatever was said to me.

I had a conversation with myself and told myself "the next time someone compliments you, know that you are worthy of the compliment so simply just say "THANK YOU." The first couple times I failed at it but I kept trying. I also started complimenting myself out loud in the mirror. We can see others and it becomes easier to compliment them. But it's time to look at yourself and compliment you. So, the next time someone compliments you just simply say THANK YOU.

Self-Love Exercise: Go to the mirror right now. Look at yourself and find five things to compliment yourself on. Write down the five things you complimented yourself on. This maybe challenging but you can do it.
Remember to tell yourself I AM ENOUGH

1.

2.

3.

4.

5.

Self-Love Journal Exercise: Think about the thoughts and feeling you felt while looking at yourself in the mirror.

Write down your thoughts and feelings. Also take the time to think about the compliments you gave yourself, journal the thoughts you chose.

Admire Yourself Daily

When admiring other people's gardens, don't forget to tend to your own flowers
-Sandkar Khan

Day 4 Admire Yourself

Webster defines Admire as "regard (an object, quality, or person) with respect or warm approval. "

With social media, we have the ability to see the lives of people, whereas in times past we would not have access to them in that way. We live our lives in front of the world. It is easy to view the life of other people and pick out the things that you admire about others. We admire people for so many reasons without having access to the full details of what it took for them to become who or what they are. We spend countless hours watching the life of others and very little time looking at ourselves.

Taking the time to get to know you better. Loving you is about learning yourself. Being able to identify the many amazing qualities that you possess and cultivate them. I heard someone once say "the grass is greener on the side if you water it."

Feelings less than and not equal to those you admire can be a direct reflect of your inability to see how gifted, talented, artistic, smart and simply amazing you are.

In my process, learning to love myself required me to accept myself for who I am and where I currently am in life. I also had to learn to be okay with what I am and what I'm not. Once I started loving me for me, the lives of others became secondary to who I am and the person I wanted to become. I started speaking out loud in the mirror the things I admire about me. The more I spoke it to myself the more I believed it and, in the process, I identified that I am valuable.

Self-Love Exercise: In the definition of Admire there are some key words that sticks out to me.

Regard, Quality, Respect, Warm Approval

Think about the person you admire the most.

Name:_____

Why do you regard them?

What qualities do they have?

What about them do you respect?

Why does their life get a warm approval?

Now take the time to think about you. Do you have any of those things you admire about them? Yes or No

Self-Love Journal Exercise: Based on your answer, journal about the way you feel about the things you identified or those things that were missing. In order to fix it you have to identify it. Learning to love you is about identifying the things about you that you love and admire.

Come up with your own list of things you admire about YOU

Invest in yourself:

- Meditate
- Read
- Eat healthy food
- Drink water
- Move your body
- Spend time in nature
- Rest up

-YOU ARE WORTHY

Day 5 Invest in You

As a child I was always told to be kind to others. To give to others and take time to serve others. To be careful with our words to others because words hurt. This was good teaching because we should do all of those things. But no one told me to that I should be kind to myself. To be careful with what I said to myself. To give to myself and serve myself. So, I mastered being to others what I wasn't to myself.

In 2009, I found myself empty with nothing left for me or anyone else. I had given to everyone but gave nothing to myself. I was in a very low place and I was hopeless and felt worthless for years. It wasn't until 2012 I decided I was going to invest in me. I was going to give myself permission to invest in me. I discovered that I am my best for others when I am my best for me.

I wanted to look better, feel better and be better. I wanted to do better with how I treated me.

I discovered in a counseling session with my therapist that I needed to set time aside for me in order to be mentally and physically healthy. I loved to take bubble baths so my therapist suggested that I scheduled them in my daily schedule. I wanted to lose weight so I hired a personal trainer. I started journaling my thoughts to get them out my head and I learned the good, the bad and the ugly about me and I embraced it. I learned that I AM WORTH THE INVESTMENT.

Self-Love Exercise: Invest in yourself by doing daily self-care. Identify what you enjoy and do it. Identify what helps you to mentally, physically and spiritually reset. If you are having trouble figuring it out here are some ways you can invest in YOU!!

Meditate

Read

Make healthy meal choices

Drink more water

Minimize your screen time

Go for a walk

Spend time in nature

Get some rest

Journal

These are just suggestion but find what resets you. You are worthy of the investment in you.

Self-Love Journal Exercise: Write out a plan on how you will invest more of your time in YOU!!!!

"To forgive is to set a prisoner free and discover that the prisoner was YOU"

— Lewis Smedes

Day 6 Forgive You

Have you ever been hurt? No, I mean like really. I mean the hurt that just takes your breath away. I have more times than I can count. Repeatedly for years by someone who I loved but for 19 years and that said they loved me. After 19 year of marriage I found myself hurt and broken and it was not my fault. The hurt left me angry and I thought I had the right to be angry and I wore it as a badge.

After the separation I was able to move pass the drastic change in my life and begin to live again. Then one day my best friend asked me if I was over the hurt and my response was "Absolutely" and her follow up question changed the course of my life. She asked "When you talk about it, does it still hurt?" I answered her yes, it will always hurt and she said "you're not over if you haven't forgiven him."

That rocked my world and forced me to face the fact that I had imprisoned myself with unforgiveness. I realize that I was trapped and holding on to the pain of what happened to me. I was hurt rightfully so, but if I was going to be chained to the pain then I should save myself the trouble of starting over and just stay in the marriage.

It was then I started on a journey learning how to forgive and the more I did the better I felt. I started looking inward and figuring out what part I played in my pain? Figuring out how did I help him hurt me? When did I stop being a victim and started being a participator in my pain? I realized I needed to take ownership of my part in the matter and it started with first forgiving myself and then forgiving him.

Forgiveness isn't for the person who did you wrong it is for you. Carrying the anger, guilt and pain is heavy on your heart and can show up in every area of your life. Forgiveness is a choice and you have to make a decision to forgive. You don't just wake up and it's done, you must decide to do the work to forgive. It will make all the difference in your life. It is like taking off the chains that have you bond. You are free to live and to breathe again. It's like taking the weights off and being able to progress in life free from being hindered by your past.

Self-Love Exercise: The first step to walking in forgiveness and no longer being chained to your pain is simply to forgive yourself. Often, we hold ourselves hostage. There is a hostage situation and you are both victim and villain. So, take some time and start to think about the things and areas in your life where you need to simply forgive YOU. It's difficult to really love you if you haven't forgiven you.

In my book Frozen: My Journey to True Forgiveness, I talk about a coaching model that I created The 3 A's. Accept, Acknowledge, Adjust. **Accept** the fact that you need to forgive you, **Acknowledge** what you could have done differently, and **Adjust** by taking the action to forgiving YOU.

Self-Love Journal Exercise: In your journal, write yourself an apology letter. Be very specific about what you are apologizing for. This is going to be emotional and it is going to require you to dig a little, but it will be well worth it.

You never fully see how toxic someone is until you breathe fresher air.

© NotSalmon.com

Day 7 Rid Yourself of Toxic People

Looking back at life from 1993-2012. I didn't realize how toxic my life was. It didn't dawn on me how the toxic situation had crept into every space in my life. My physical, mental, emotional and financial life, had all become toxic. Not by what I did but by what I didn't do. I have discovered that when you don't protect yourself from toxics people, places and things than you give the toxicities access to consume you.

The most dangerous and one of the deadliest, are the toxics that seep in undetected. The ones that come in and you didn't see them, feel them, or even smell them before your realized what has been taken place and it's too late.

These unseen toxins come into our life in many ways. One of the ways is becoming connected in one way or another with a toxic relationship. When you are connected in relationship you become what they are whether you want to or not. It is impossible for you to jump in water without getting wet in the same way you can't be in relationship with a toxic person without becoming toxic.

When I decided to end my first marriage, it was because I realized how deadly it was to my well-being, I severed the tie that had me bound and connected me to him. And for the first time since being a teenager I could breathe.

The haze of toxics that hovered over my life dissipated. I could finally breathe again. Life became one fresh breathe after the other. The stress of what it required me to sacrifice to maintain the toxic relationship gave was for me to be able to see life in a different way. Finally, I could breathe.

Self-Love Exercise: Start to examine your ties, covenants, connections in every area of your life and examine it according to the definitions of toxic- Capable of causing death, exhibiting symptoms of infections, extremely harsh, malicious or harmful relating to or being an asset that has lost so much value that it cannot be sold on the market. Causes something to be devalued. If you find any of these things present in your current relationships, reconsider it and what is it costing you to be connected. Love yourself enough to detox from your toxic connections.

Self-Love Journal Exercise: Start to create a detox in your life and space. A detox is a regimen or treatment intended to remove toxins and impurities from your body, mind and spirit. Write out in your journal.

1. What is toxic in your life?

2. Who is toxic in your life?

3. What makes you feel like you are suffocating?

4. Who are you connected to that cost you more to just be connected to?

5. Who contaminates your peace?

After taking time to journal your answers the write out a plan to detox.

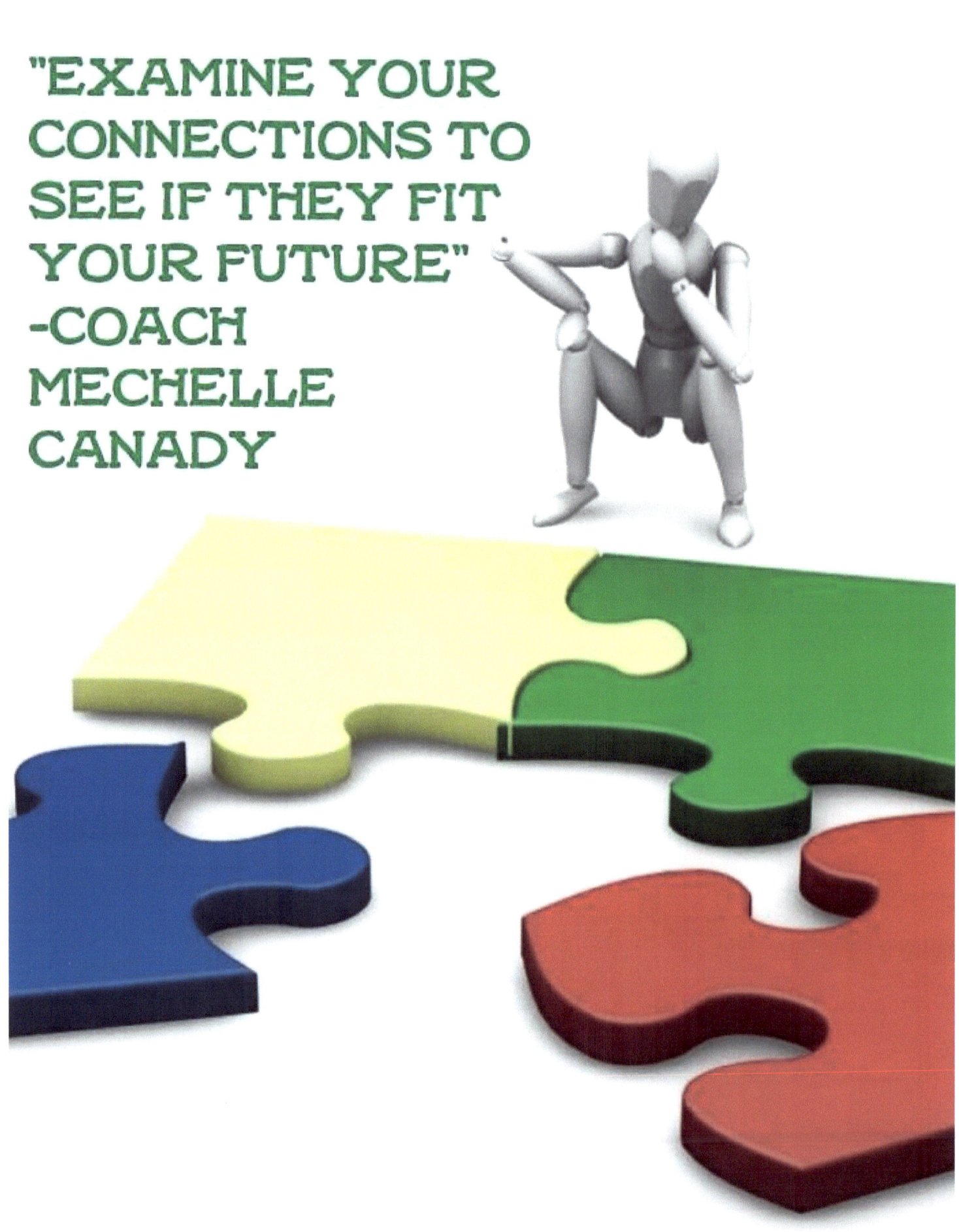

Day 8 Examine Your Connections

My mother grows flowers. She truly has a real green thumb. It's like she can take a leaf off of any plant and grow another plant from it. She is the only person I know who can take the plants you get from the funeral and grow them. My mom has plants in her front room that she's had for twenty years. They just keep growing and growing until they hit the roof of the house. She has mastered the art of growing plants.

She loves her plants. She talks to the them, feed them and she has even given them names. She gives them bottled water and placed them out to get sun and rain water. She really treats them like family.

You may be thinking what does my momma having a green thumb has to do with examining connection? In her process of loving her plants she realized that as much as she loves them there is a time before the next season that she has to prune the leaves that are no longer suitable for the next season. So, in your Journey of Self-Love, it's time to start to examine your connections.

There are connections that will not be suitable for the you now that you LOVE YOU. My momma didn't just cut any and every leaf on the plants but she examines to see which ones are no longer green and no longer growing. She looks to see which leaves have already died and are not vibrant and flourishing. Those are the ones she cut. Where she cuts them is strategic. She cut them off without causing damage to the plant so that the growth isn't affected for the next season.

There will also be connections in your life that you will need to cultivate and help to grow. When my mom completes the pruning of her plants, she would take time to care for the plant to create an environment for growth. She would turn the dirt to stir up the nutrients, she adds more dirt and fertilizer to give the plants the additional minerals needed to grow for the next season. Those you are connected to that are healthy or just needs a littler help growing, see how you can fertilize and build the connection up to be a vital relationship that adds value and will help to propel you to the next dimension in your life.

Love yourself enough to disconnect and prune your connections so that you are not frustrated and weighed down with bad and toxic connections and create an atmosphere of growth in those relationships that will help you in the next season of your life.

It is vital that you examine and understand the importance of this in your life. Holding on to people who should be cut lose will stop you from growing at the pace you are capable of growing.

Love yourself enough to do a true evaluation of who you are connected to, and if they fit your future. If they don't love you enough do not be afraid let them go.

Self-Love Exercise: Write down your top 10 qualities. Write down your top 5 connections. Start to analyze your connections to see if your top 5 exemplify any of those qualities. Do your top 5 connections build up your qualities or tear them down? Do they add value to your life? This reflection should start you to thinking about who you should keep and who you should disconnect from.

Self-Love Journal Exercise: Come up with a plan to enhance the connections you are going to keep. Write what you can do to cultivate the connection. Write out how they add value to you and also how you can add value to them. Now that you have done the pruning it is time to cultivate.

CREATING HEALTHY BOUNDARIES

"Guard your heart above all else, for it determines the course of your life"

Proverbs 4:23

Day 9 Set Healthy Relationship Boundaries

Boundaries are like laws put in place to keep you safe. In life it is very important to set healthy relationship boundaries to keep your heart safe. In life just as there are laws of the land, there should be laws for your life. When I realized who Mechelle had become, I discovered it was because I had no boundaries in place to keep me protected from hurt harm and danger. Those who I was connected to in my life had free reign in how they handled me, treated me and dealt with me on all levels.

I gave to those who I love and those I led 100% of me. You may be thinking why is this wrong to give 100% of you? Well if you are giving 100% of you to others what is left for yourself? I found myself in the lowest point in my life completely empty. I served others at the highest level within my power because I thought it was right. I thought I was doing something great by being all in at all times. Any time people would ask me to do something, whether I wanted to or not I did it and for me I don't know how to do anything on a normal level. So, I gave, gave and gave until I was all the way empty. When I found myself in the empty place, I also discovered I was alone. I could not call on any of those people who I gave all of me to for help.

Once I had come to my senses, I realized I needed to recreate a new me and put some parameters in place so that I never get back in that place ever again. I knew I did not want to feel the way I was feeling and I also knew in order for me to not be in that place again, I needed to do things differently.

The first change I implemented was the word "NO". My business partner Coach Jae Smith says "No is a complete sentence." No doesn't require anything else, no reason nor an explanation. I walked around most of my life feeling overwhelmed because I thought I was supposed to tell everyone yes. If I said no, they would not like me or even love me. I had that sister-girl superwomen mentality. I was really trying to be every woman but I had nothing left for me. I was the go-to girl, the one everyone called on but when I needed me for me, I couldn't show up for me.

We are granted grace for our life. We are given what is needed to be able to carry the weight of our on personal trials. We get in trouble when we allow others to impose upon us their issues, problems and trials.

Secondly, I set standards for what was going to be acceptable and what would not. I set relationship boundaries, boundaries for my family and for myself. These standards served as boundaries. These standards helped me to safeguard my heart from mistreatment from others and from myself.

Lastly, I realized that I set the standard, the laws and boundaries for my life. Once I set the expectation of what was acceptable, people started realizing that in order to be in my space they had to govern themselves accordingly.

In this journey of learning self, you will quickly learn that self-preservation is the key to loving you. Love yourself enough to take care of your well-being first. When you fly, the pilot comes across the intercom system and gives instructions. One of the instructions he gives is in the event that the oxygen mask comes down, you are instructed to apply your own mask first and then help others. You are no good to others if you are not any good to yourself. Love those around you enough to love you first.

Think of your boundaries like gates. Gates are made to keep things in and keep things out. The gates will keep what is behind the gates safe and secure and will keep it undisturbed by whats is on the outside of the gates. Protect you by putting up those healthy boundaries and do not sacrifice yourself trying to preserve others.

Set boundaries, healthy boundaries by guarding your heart.

Self-Love Exercise:

- Think about the areas in your life you feel most overwhelmed in. Write them down.
- Think about the areas of your life you feel exhausted about. Write them down.
- Think about the last time you did something for someone that you really did not want to do. Write it down.
- Think about the people in your life that cost you too much to be connected with them. Write them down.
- Think about the people who make you feel you have been used. Write them down.
- Think about how much of you do you give to you. Write them down.

Self-Love Journal Exercise:

Take some time and write out your thoughts and feelings about where you have boundaries already in placed in your life but also write about those areas where boundaries need to be in place. Take time to write out how you can do things differently when it comes to establishing boundaries.

Write out your NO statement- the next time someone is requiring more of you than you are willing to give them. Remember NO is a complete sentence. It requires nothing else. No reason, No explanation.

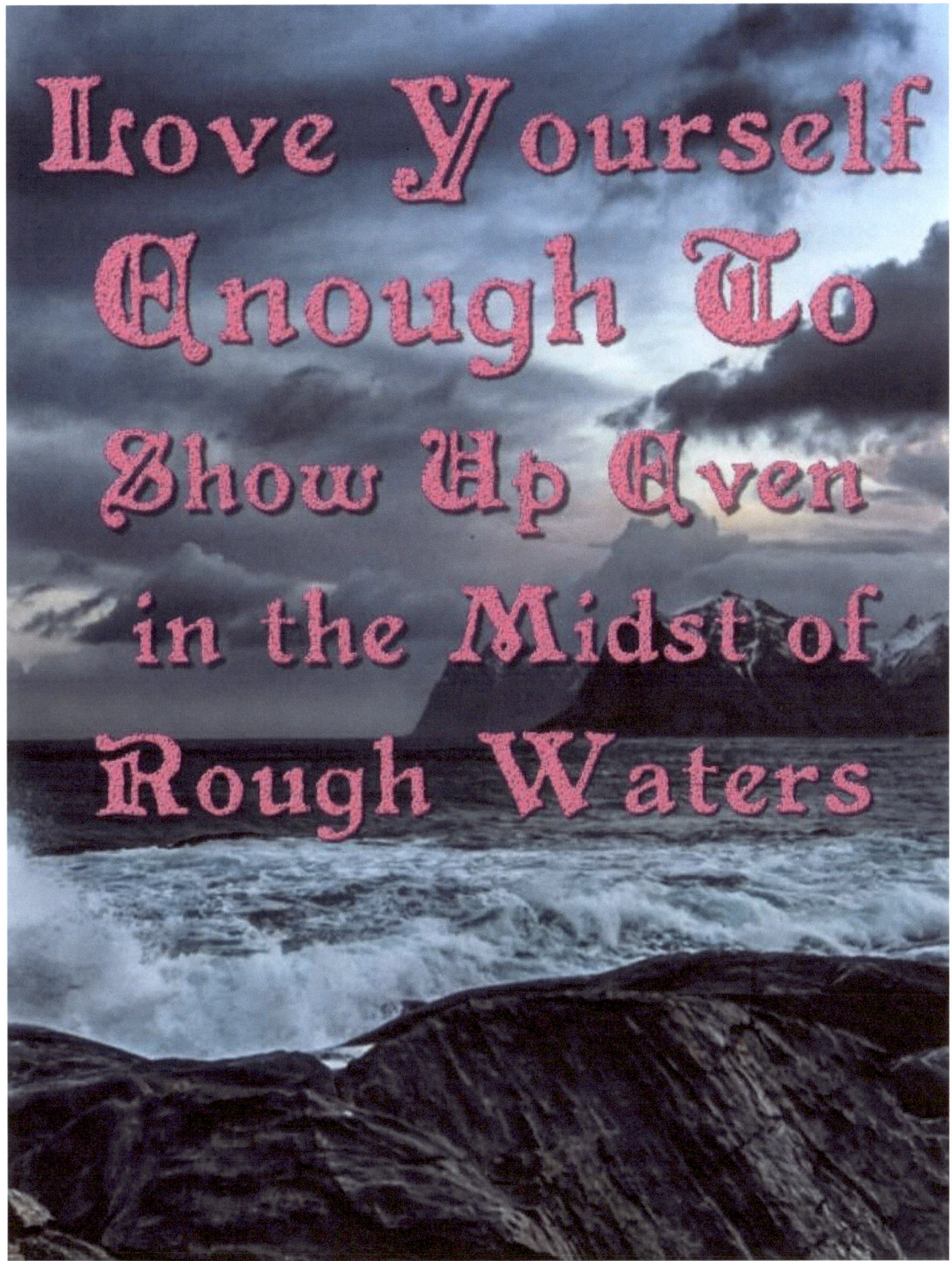

Day 10 to Show Up for You

I have come to the realization that always being available for others can leave you too tired to fight for yourself. I found myself in that place. I was so busy being present for everyone else that I could not be present for me. I needed me and I had nothing to give me.

2009 is when I realized I was empty and depressed. I needed to stop giving so much of me out to others and start practicing self-preservation. Definition of self-preservation. 1 : preservation of oneself from destruction or harm. 2 : a natural or instinctive tendency to act so as to preserve one's own existence. So, in other words SAVE YOU FIRST.

Again, when you are flying the captain will come over the intercom and will instruct you. "If your oxygen mask comes down, APPLY YOURS FIRST and then help others." If you are no good to you then you are no good to anyone else.

We have been given a measure of grace for what we have to go through and what we have to endure. We become overwhelmed and are unable to show up for ourselves when we have taken on the problems, issues, and responsibilities of others. You have not been equipped to take on the problems of others. You can be there to show support and help others through what they are going through but it is not your job to take on the burdens of others. When carrying the weight of others, it leaves you no room to carry your own. When it is time for you to fight for yourself you will have no fight left. Love yourself enough to save some of you for you.

In order for you to be able to be present for you in the midst of rough waters you have to make sure you are taking care of you. Make sure you are mentally stable enough to be present in your own situation. Have you ever been so loaded down with the problems of others that when your storm started raging you felt like you were sinking and just gave up on your struggle? You couldn't fight your fight because there was nothing left. Are you at the point of giving up on you because you feel you can't fight anymore? **Don't lay down on the fight!! Remember the definition.** 2 : a natural or instinctive tendency to act so as to preserve one's own existence. Don't give up SHOW UP FOR YOU.

Self-Love Exercise:

Here are 5 steps to follow review them over and over again until they become a part of you thought process.

Step 1- Start from today

Step 2- Give everybody back their own problems you don't have the grace for it

Step 3- Only give to others your overflow

Step 4- Don't lay down on the fight

Step 5- Don't give up on you

Self-Love Journal Exercise:

Take a few minutes and think about the ways you have over extended yourself to others. Think about the moments of you felt overwhelmed and what brought you to that point. After taking some time to think about it, then start writing a promissory note to yourself to not get to that point again. Promise yourself to always look out for you and be there for you in the times that you need you.

If it has already happen YOU CAN'T UNHAPPEN IT

Day 11 You Can't Unhappen It

Living in regret of past situations can hold you hostage. Decisions you made, where to go, what to do, who to love, and who not to love will plague your life and steal moments of your right now. Past failures will deflate your esteem, trust and your ego and make you not want to try again.

Then there are past mistakes in relationships that will affect the way you deal with people. You can really damage your present by the past hurts and disappointments. You can also damage healthy relationships when you are handling the person as if they are the person from the past. You can't UNHAPPEN hurts of your past so don't let it cause you to reenact it into your present.

I personally have made some not so smart and some plain ole dumb decisions in my life. Ones that my family and friends told me not to make, yet I did them anyway and paid dearly for it. They all had consequences and repercussions that I am still paying for to this day. But I have been able to move forward by forgiving myself, learning the lessons in my mistake and realizing that there is nothing I can do that will allow me to go back and change what I did. I can't UNHAPPEN it.

It's like a glass, if you break a glass and glue it back together no matter how perfect you line the glass up and glue it together, you will still see the cracks. It might hold water the same as it did before it was cracked but you can't uncrack it. That's the way your decisions of your past are. You are here today so you survived the mistakes of your past. You were able to put yourself back together again. You can even be made whole again but you can't UNHAPPEN what was done, but you can still be used and the hurts of your past can be your greatest testimonies.

I was able to forgive myself and get past my not so great decisions in life by one simple practice called the 3A's Accept, Acknowledge, and Adjust.

I had to Accept the fact that I could not go back and change what I had already done. I can't UNHAPPEN it. Accept the fact that I needed to make better choices and Accept the fact that I didn't make the best decision for my future.

Secondly, Acknowledge was the next step. I needed to take ownership and of my part in the failure of my marriage. Even though I wasn't the one who was per say doing the wrong of cheating, lying, stealing, he was. But I had a part in it because I allowed him to continue to do those things to me. So, I didn't stop him from hurting me. I wasn't a victim I was a participant. Once I acknowledge I was partly at fault, I looked at the situation differently.

Adjust was the last and final step. Since I had already accepted that change needed to happen, acknowledge what went wrong and my part in it, I now needed to do something about it. My adjustment was seeking healings. I realized I can't get healed the same place I got hurt. I needed to in spite of my fear of the unknown or my fear of what will happen next, I had to change my environment. I literally packed up and moved. The adjust process is the "DO SOMETHING" phase. I realized that I can't UNHAPPEN it so I needed to do something about it. You can do the same by Accept, Acknowledge, Adjust!!!

Self-Love Exercise: Go to the mirror look yourself in the eyes and tell yourself "YOU CAN'T UNHAPPEN IT."

Self-Love Journal Exercise: Think about the things that hold you back from progressing and moving forward from your past. On the journal page write down on separate line ACCEPT, ACKNOWLEDGE, ADJUST. Now write it out and let the healing begin.

EXAMINE YOUR CIRCLE

FOLLOWERS
FANS
FRIENDS

Day 12 Know Who Your Friends Are

Putting people in place in your life, will elevate most disappointments with those who are in your inner circle. There are times when your inner circle doesn't provide you with what you currently need. We become very frustrated when we have people in the wrong place of our life. In doing so our expectations of the role they are expected to fulfill is off and we lose good people because we become frustrate with the unmet expectations.

There are 3 roles that we can put the people in our circle in, Followers, Fans, Friends.

Let's define the three roles. First Followers- those who trail you from a distance. They "follow" you on social media, they like your post from time to time, and occasionally comment on your post, but nothing else. If you have not identified that the person is a follower only you might find yourself disappointed and feeling unsupported if you are looking for them to show up at an engagement or purchase your product. You will find yourself discouraged if you are looking for all the people who "follow" to be present for you. They don't have your heart nor vision in mind so don't be mistaken in thinking they will do anything other than "follow" you from a distance. They don't provide real support they only provide numbers. They never provide real engagement but they are maintaining a watch on what you are doing. They won't show up for you, won't be significant in any way in your life, they are just around. Your followers will also watch to report to those who don't have access to watch. Does this sound like anyone you know? Followers have no benefit but they are needed.

Secondly, Fans- Now these are the ones who are more interactive. They want to have a closer seat in the arena of your life. They will support you but the support is limited. They will show up for the easy stuff. They show up when things are going well in your life. As long as they are able to gather from you what they want or what they need, they are around. You can only give them access to your pretty picture. Your fans won't show up at your event but they will share your flyer!! They will tell someone about your product and they will refer someone to you from time to time. Identifying those who are your Fans will help you put them in perspective in your life. Because knowing their capacity to be a Fan will limit the frustration and disappointment in them. If you are expecting more from people than they are willing or have the capacity to provide will cause you to be hurt, disappointed and also at time angry.

Your role in a person's life may not be their role in your life so be clear in what role people play in your life to avoid ending good relationships due to misplacement.

Lastly, Friend- Webster defines a friend as a person whom one knows and with whom one has a bond of mutual affection. So, in an essence to be a friend there need to be a mutual bond or mutual affection. These are the people who support you like you support them; they participate in your life, they show up for you when you need them, they support what you do and things you are a part of. We generally don't have a lot of people who fall in this category. The closer to the middle the smaller the circle gets. That is why it is totally possible to have 100,000 followers on social media and feel completely alone. We need friends in our lives who want nothing more from us than to be our friend. These are the ones that will tell you are when you wrong and help you see things from another perspective. They will help get you back on track when you have fallen down. These are the ones you can fall out with on Monday morning and they calling you at lunch to make a lunch date. True friends are few far and between. Friends will allow you to be who you truly are and still love you for who you are.

Misplacement of people will cause you undue pain and suffering because you want from them what they can't give you. Its like putting a square peg in a circle it just doesn't fit.

Self-Love Exercise: List your top 5 people you communicate with on a regular bases and decide which category they fit.

1.

2.

3.

4.

5.

Self-Love Journal Exercise: Start to evaluate the roles that you play in others life that you are in connection with. Start to think more and more about the way you interact with them and journal your experience. You may discover that you are in the wrong place in some people lives.

KNOW THE CAPACITY OF THOSE IN YOUR CIRCLE! EVERYONE CANT HANDLE YOUR CAPACITY

Day 13 Know the Capacity of Those Around You

Loving You is learning how to protect yourself from undue stress, aggravation and frustration that comes from being in a relationship with yourself and relationship with others. We spend a lot of time and effort expecting from people what they don't have the capacity to provide. We also spend time inwardly frustrated not knowing or understanding our own capacity. Knowing your own capacity of what you can do, can't do, can handle and can't handle. We must know what triggers us to do good or what triggers us to shut down. Not having a good understanding of your thresholds brings about frustration when expectations are not met. Most disappointments are directly connected to unmet expectations. When our expectations aren't met, we are often disappointed and our feelings get hurt. When we know the capacity, our expectations change. It's like if you have a gallon of water and a bottle of water, they both have the same content but can hold a different amount. So, if you pour a bottle of water into an empty gallon that leaves a lot of room in the gallon jug. But if you take a gallon of water and attempt to pour the gallon of water into the water bottle it doesn't have the ability or capacity to hold the water. That's how our life is oftentimes, we are the gallon of water and those in our circle is the bottles of water. You can handle their capacity with ease and room to spare but they are unable to handle yours. When we expect ordinary people to perform at an extraordinary level, we are let down. We expect from people what we give to them. Well they don't have the capacity to give that back to us.

So, we find ourselves irritated, agitated, frustrated. When we expect ordinary people to give back to us the extraordinary that we've given them. They don't have the ability to provide to you what you gave to them. I remember at a point in my life I was very disappointed in people and I picked up the motto of no expectation; no disappointment. This allowed me to accept people for who they are and for where they are. For years I did not connect with people simply because I had nothing I could give to people because I had given away to people what I could not get back from them. But the truth of the matter is, they didn't have the capacity to give me back what I gave to them.

Once I started to live by the no expectations; no disappointment mantra, I could truly see people for who they really are and I can meet them where they really are. It's like if you agree to pick someone up from a particular location and you arrived there and they are not there that's what happens between us and people. We expect to meet people in the place of extraordinary, so they are not where we expected them to be because they are at ordinary. So, get rid of the preconceived notion of what people should do back for you for what you do for them. This will change your life and set you free from disappointment and let down. No this does not free people from accountability. People must be accountable for what they are and what they do but what it does is take a load off you when they don't do what they never had the ability to do.

Maya Angelou said "when people show you who they are believe them." We often see people in a different light than they really are and we want better for people then they want for themselves. Just like you have to acknowledge where you currently are, you also have to acknowledge where the people around you currently are. Knowing the capacity of those around you takes away the undue expectation of people to be perfect and to always get it right but when there's no expectation there's no disappointment and you can love people for who they really are.

Self-Love Exercise: Write down on a sticky note "No expectations; No disappointments." Make it visible for you to see and as often as you need to remind yourself in those tough situations in relationship.

Self-Love Journal Exercise: take a moment and think about the last time you were disappointed by unmet expectations.

KNOW HOW MUCH OF YOU TO GIVE TO THOSE AROUND YOU. NOT EVERYONE IS EQUIPPED TO HANDLE THE FULL YOU

Day 14 Everyone Can't Handle All of You

One day I was watching TEDx UNO video and I came across a video titled "5 People You Need in Your Life to be Happy" by Stacey Flowers. This video talks about you being the average of the 5 people closes to you. This video really caused me to review those around me.

The 5 key people she discussed is
A cheerleader who roots you on
A mentor who points you in the right direction
A coach who helps to guide you
A friend who helps to comfort you
A coworker relates to you in your work or you field

These are your factor 5 and it doesn't have to be 5 actual people but the roles are what's important. We sometimes expect our best friend to be our all and when they can't fulfill the roles, we are left disappointed because they didn't meet our expectations. Knowing the capacity of those around you is about knowing what part of you they speak to. Disappointment comes when expectations are not met. You don't expect a tree to be a dog nor do you expect your dog to be a tree. Your expectations for the dog are to run, jump, bark and the tree to produce shade, fruit and to be grounded. Now the same is with those around you in your tribe.

You may be thinking what does this have to do with me loving myself. But it absolutely does and here it goes. Love yourself enough not to give people the wrong parts of you. Giving them what they can handle and it will bring you success and joy. It saves you disappointment, hard feelings and from ruining good relationships. You're not convinced yet? Okay I got you. I have a friend who whenever I come up with one of my brilliant idea, I can call her and she is going to tell me how wonderful my idea is, how smart I am and how no one in the world is as smart as me. She is my cheerleader and has been for years. I work in the fraud department of a national bank and sometimes my job can be absolutely stressful. I was riding home one day and decided to call her to vent about my day. I called her and I gave her an ear full and more. She quietly listened and said nothing the entire time I talked. Our conversation is never one-sided we interrupt each other and go back and forth but this time it was different. Once I was finished all she said was WOW. Nothing else. I was completely lost and confused and a little bothered that our conversation didn't go as planned. I ended the call with my friend, saying "I'll call you later." That left me disappointed with our friendship and in my mind, I was like I won't call her anymore.

From that one situation I was ready to write off our whole friendship. Simply because at the moment it didn't dawn on me that she wasn't able to take in what I was feeling at the moment and turn it into a "cheer moment."

So, it wasn't her fault, she wasn't equipped to handle the role of my co-worker that just allowed me to just vent about my day at work. That was outside of her capacity. After taking a moment to re-evaluate my circle and their capacity of me they could handle, I am now more strategic with who I call for what I need.

Now think about how many good friendships have been ruined by not knowing your friend's capacity and what part of you they can handle!!

Self-Love Exercise: Think about your starting five friends. Those top 5 friends you have and list them. This are your top 5 go to people. Those who you go to when things are good or bad, when you are happy or sad. Those who in a situation hype you up or calm you down.

1.

2.

3.

4.

5.

Now from the 5 roles identify what capacity they serve you and list it next to their name. The next time you are in need of someone make sure you call the right one for the right job.

Cheerleader, Coach, Mentor, Friend, Coworker.

Self-Love Journal Entry: Think about your top 5 and think about times when you maybe didn't get from them what you needed at the time. Now examine their capacity and their role. I mean really think about it. What were you expecting from them and was it right to expect it from them?

Were you attempting to get from them what they didn't have the ability to give you because of their capacity?

Take some time to really think about this and you may discover that you may have lost some friendships you need to go back and mend because you were wanting them to serve you in a capacity they were not equip to.

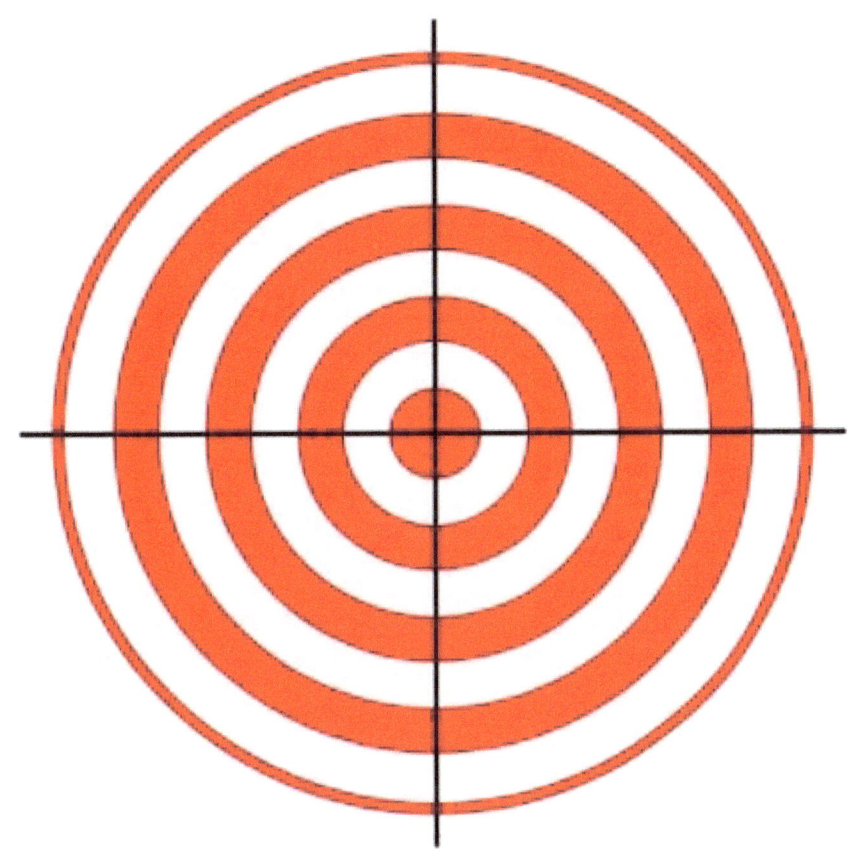

Take the time to find out what Centers YOU

Day 15 Find Out What Centers You

In this day and age of technology, your charger for your devices such as phones, tablets, and laptops has become essential to your life. I remember when I was growing up there was an American Express commercial and at the end of the commercial, they would say "And never leave home without it." That is the way we feel about our chargers, we never leave home without it. Because our devices are essential to our life we feel we need to be connected. You make sure you charge your device; you do updates to your device and you restart your phone to get everything aligned and reset. Because in order for your device to function properly there are steps that's needed to ensure it continues to function.

Now we take all of these measures to make sure that when we need to use our devices, they are charged but we fail to make sure we are charged. We allow ourselves to get drained and run down. We allow ourselves to give out so much that we find ourselves on empty. When your battery is dead your phone is not good for use and neither are you uncharged.

I found myself empty in 2009. I had given out everything I had to give. I was so many things to so many people, I had nothing left for myself. We will be of no value to anyone until we love ourselves enough to figure out what centers us.

I went to see a psychiatrist because I was on the verge of having another mental breakdown. He said to me you need to take some time to center you. You are over extending yourself in what you give to others and it is leaving nothing for yourself. If you don't do something to correct it you are going to end up back in the mental hospital.

For me that was a big wake up call. I know how it felt being in the mental hospital trying to figure out I got up there. With tons of questions and with no answers.

I didn't want to go through that again, so I needed to figure out how to fix it. I decided that I would start doing self-care and figure out what centered me.

I realized that for the majority of my day my time was spent with people. My spouse, my kids, my church members, my employees and never just me. I started by carving out time of my day just for me. I discussed my need to have some me time with my family and they helped me to navigate through it. I started journaling my thoughts and feelings to get it all out of my mind and on paper.

Fast forward 10 years to now, I am working a full-time job and running my businesses full time. I have so many people I serve as a life coach too, but yet there are times that I feel myself getting low and I must take time to center me. I have developed what I called "my reset." My reset is what gets me balanced, centered, refilled and ready to take on the world. I have deemed Mondays as my reset day. Now you may not be able to take a whole day to reset but it is very necessary that you take some time for you. It is not the quantity of time but the quality of time.

I also do not just center my body by reset, I center my spirit through corporate worship, meditation, prayer, and inspirational videos to help me center my soul and my spirit. This keeps my moral compass centered, keeps me on the right track in all areas of life. I have affirmations all around my house to keep me visually and mentally centered and reminded of my goals, mission, and tasks.

It's not an easy task because we are taught to see about others and that seeing about us is selfish. No, it isn't selfish it is necessary. We must practice self-preservation. Once again like when you are on the plane and the captain comes on the overhead and says "in the event that the mask come down due to turbulence APPLY YOUR MASK FIRST AND THEN ATTEMPT TO HELP OTHERS". So, when it comes to your own self-care apply it to you and then apply it to others. Save you first.

Self-Love Exercise: Go to the mirror, look yourself in the eyes and apologize for putting others first and not making sure you are first. Have a conversation with yourself about the changes that is needed on a daily bases to ensure you are a priority.

Self-Love Journal Exercise: Set a plan for 7days to take time to reset daily. Identify what that reset looks like. Here is a list of self-care regimens to help you center yourself and get recharged,

1. Pick one thing that you need to do and get it done so it's off your mental "to do" list.
2. Get a manicure or pedicure.
3. Get a massage.
4. Spend a few minutes each day learning something new.
5. Use a planner or a calendar to intentionally schedule "me time."
6. Listen to music that inspires.
7. Listen to a video that motivates you.
8. Drink calming tea and curl up with a good book.
9. Write a list of things you're grateful to have in your life and post it somewhere you can see it often.
10. Journal it out

SSSHHH

SILENCE YOUR INNER CRITIC
YOU CAN
YOUR ARE READY
YOU ARE QUALIFIED
YOU ARE A WINNER
YOU ARE NOT A FAILURE
YOU WILL

Day 16 Silence Your Inner Critic

Growing up there was a cartoon titled GI Joe: The Great American Hero. At the end of the cartoon GI Joe always ended the show by saying "knowing is half the battle." Many of us lose battles daily simply because we don't know that we are in a battle. Knowing that you are in a fight is half of what's needed to win the battle. We lose our personal struggles because we don't understand that we are in a daily battle. We are in a battle against our thoughts, against the words that have been said to us and by us. Knowing that there is a battle going on in your head to a point that your failures or your success begin in your mind first. We do things twice, first in our head before it is manifested in life. There is a quote that says "don't be pushed around by the fears in your mind." Don't allow your thoughts and failures and thoughts of failure to push you around. Don't allow the thoughts of failure and not actual failure dictate what you do. The battlefield in the mind is where most battles are fought, won and lost, but if you don't know that you are warring against those words and your mind, you're losing every day. The inner critic inside your head is always fighting against you.

We are our hardest critics; we are our biggest critics. You have to learn to silence the inner critic. You also have to learn to give it a positive word to give to yourself. The more you put in positive the more positive comes out your mouth and in your mind. In the bible David had to encourage himself daily.

Your mind is always telling you that you can't, you're not ready, you're not qualified, you're a failure, you're a loser, and you won't. But start today telling yourself "YOU CAN." You have the ability to take charge of what you are thinking. You can't control your thoughts but you can control what you are thinking. Start declaring that you can do it, declaring that you will do it, declaring that you are winner, declaring that you will no longer lose, and your power lies in you. You have the power to be everything you need to be successful because it already lies within you. Be determined to not lose the battle in your mind before you actually fight the battle. Silence the inner critic. Managing your self-talk is the key to success. Your inner critic is always going to tell you that you can't when on

the side you have the power to do decide today that you are going to stop being and start doing.

That moment when you think you have done a great job at something and then that voice in your head picks you apart. That's the voice of your inner critic. I gave my inner critic a name. Her name is Petty Penelope. I named her Petty Penelope because she is PETTY. She will pick me apart. I have felt like I was on the mountain top and by the time she is done being petty, I am in the valley. The words she says to me sometimes are so cruel. But I realize a lot of what she says to me sounds a lot like what other people have said to me. She repeats to me the unkind things that has been said to me but she repeats it in my voice. So, what others have said to hurt me is now being used by me on me.

We can't control what comes to our mind but we can control what we do with those thoughts. You can't control your thoughts but you can control what you think.

The first step to overcoming your inner critic is identifying the voice of your inner critic. Then counter acting the negative thoughts by controlling your self-talk. The key to winning is knowing that there is a battle going on. Knowing is half the battle.

Self-Love Exercise: Throughout the day today, keep track of all the negative thoughts that comes to your mind. Write them down and make notes of what you say to you.

Self-Love Journal: Getting to understand your Inner Critic is acknowledging the voice of your inner critic and being counter active to the negative things you say to you. From your list of things that your inner critic, identify who said it to you first. By identifying where it came from, you can counter act it by declaring the opposite.

PRICELESS
10000000000000000000000000000000000000000000000000000000

LEARN YOUR VALUE AND LET NO ONE DISCOUNT IT!!!

Day 17 Know Your Worth

Only the manufacturer of a thing can speak to the true value of a thing. The manufacturer knows the time, the tools, the resources, and the products that were needed to make a thing. In order to create something, the manufacturer knows all the things that are on the outside of it as well as the inner workings. The manufacturer knows the true value of it because he made it.

On this journey of Self-Love, knowing your value, knowing your worth, knowing that you're Priceless, is going to be the key to others learning to value you. Items that we love, things that we value, we treat differently. There's a difference between the way you treat an item you pay little for and an item that you pay a lot for.

I love shoes so there's a difference between my everyday shoes and those shoes I keep tucked away in the closet in the shoe bag that's in the shoe box. Because I paid more and I value them more. We are no different!! Whenever you love and value someone you treat them different. You reverence them differently; you speak to them differently. It is now time that you start to Value who you are with that same energy. It is now time that you start to Value what's on the inside of you and no longer allow outside interference or outside people to determine your value. You are valuable there is no one like you. You are gifted with gifts that no one else has. You are talented and you are needed on this Earth. You are here because you are needed. You're valuable.

Take some time to think about the way you treat you. Why is it so important for you to evaluate the way you treat you, is because we teach others how to treat us by the way we treat ourselves. The way others treat us is a direct reflection of how we treat ourselves. we teach people how to value us, we are always teaching people how to treat us and how to value us and if you love you, others will love and value you. When you learn your true value; you will no longer accept those in your space who treat you less than your value. Don't let others discount you.

The purchaser of an item never determined the worth of the item. The Manufacturer provides a Suggested Retail Price. This is the least the item should be sold for based upon the value from the one who made it. This can only be determined by the maker. Psalm 139:14 says "you are fearfully and wondrously made." Stop discounting yourself!!! You don't have to change who you are to get people to like you. Embrace You. You are dope and don't dull your dopeness for anyone. You don't have to lessen who you are to get people to like you. Don't hang out in spaces you have to compete with because you are wondrously made. Don't try to put right pieces in wrong places and those who love you, value you, care for you and value being your presence.

When we value ourselves, we treat ourselves differently. People can only do to us what we allow them to do. We allow others to not treat us at a level of value we have for ourselves. Getting to know who you are, and getting to know your value will requires hard work and discipline.

I remember sitting in the library at Valdosta State University and I remember starting to make a checklist of "who am I" and what I bring to the table. It was only in making this list I learned my true value. I didn't think about what I wasn't, I didn't think about what I couldn't do. I didn't consider my size, education, or status. I thought about what Mechelle has to offer. After having that internal conversation about my value with myself, my life changed. I started handling me in a different way. I started to value and celebrate who I am. I started to have confidence in my skills, my gifts and my abilities. It was at that point that I commanded others to do so as well. Disrespect was no longer acceptable. Minimizing myself stopped being acceptable for me, devaluing myself stopped being acceptable for me. I started valuing me and I now require others to value me. It was only when I discovered my value that I could discover my true worth and the reason I should love me the way I do.

Self-Love Exercise: Below is a price tag. If you could add a monetary value to yourself what would it be? Write your value on one side of the price tag and on the other side 2 reasons you are worth that amount. When we realize that our value is on display daily in the way we walk, talk, and act, we become more aware of how we handle ourselves, our situations and circumstances.

Self-Love Journal Exercise: Take some time to journal about a recent situation when you didn't act or react according to the price on your price tag. Think about what happened and why it happened the way it did. Also, journal about how you can do things differently the next time so that you can show your value. When you display your value then others will value you.

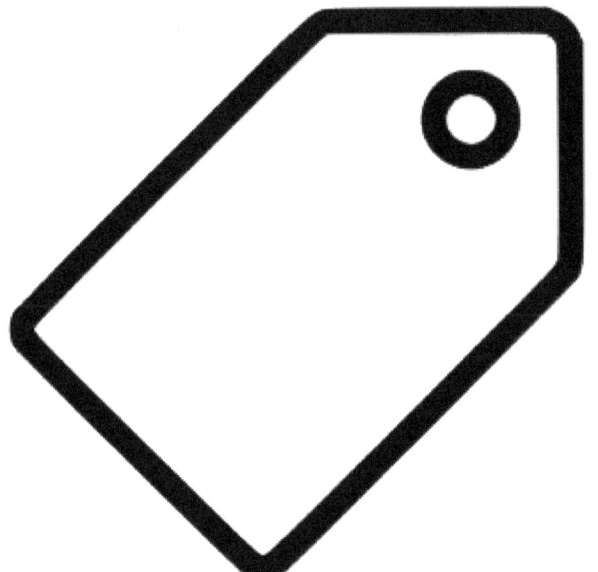 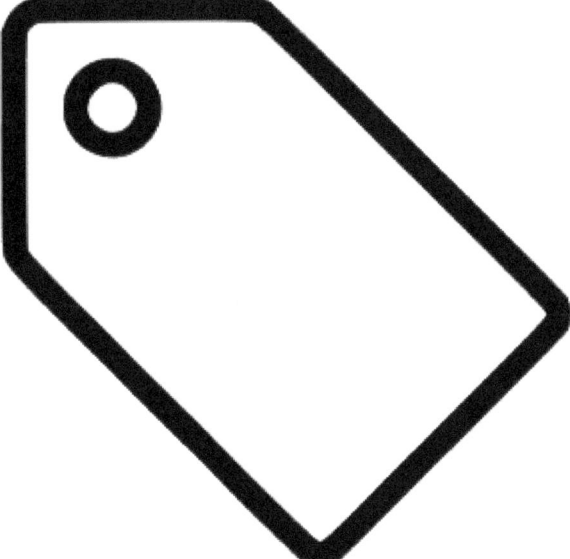

FIND YOUR PURPOSE AND PURSUE IT

Day 18 Find Your Purpose

Everything created was created with a gift inside of it. Everything that was naturally created was created with the ability to reproduce of its own kind. Everything that was created has the ability to self-sustain in the right environment without outside interference. That's the way God created everything on the Earth. When we look at the gift of the seed it's the tree inside of it. We look at the tree and see the gift of the tree is the ability to bear fruit. When we look at the fruit the gift of the fruit is the substance is it provides, and the seed inside the fruit gives it the ability to create other of its kind.

In today's society we look on the outside in order to find our purpose when our I purpose lies within. Inside of this Earthen vessel is treasures and gifts and the ability to recreate of its same kind both physically and spiritually. Your sole purpose cannot be connected to anything outside of you and who you truly are. You don't have to look at others to find out your purpose. You'll never find your true purpose looking on the outside of you. Your purpose is connected to your gifts, your purpose is connected to your ability to make others of your kind. Whatever that gift is connected to what you are supposed to leave in this earth. Gifts are given to be given away. A seed never says I'm going to keep the tree inside me because it's my gift, but it gives the gift of the tree. The tree never says I'm going to keep my fruit because it is my fruit but it gives it away. The same with you and I. We are put here on this Earth to give our gifts away.

No one takes a gift, wraps it and keeps it because it doesn't become a gift until you give it away. As long as you hold on to it, it's not a gift. Gifting doesn't happen until you do the process of giving it away. The same with your purpose, your purpose lies down within you it's not hiding. It doesn't have to be found or located; it has to be tapped into. Because it's on the inside of you, your gift and your purpose cannot be taught. Your purpose cannot be instructed. You are the only one who can make it come to pass. Your purpose here on this earth is to recreate others like you physically and spiritually. If you are not giving of your gift then you have not tapped into your purpose. Gifts are on the inside of you and cannot be compared to the gift of anyone else. There can be 100 fruit on the tree but no two fruit is truly identical, same as with your gift there may be hundreds of people with the same gift, same idea, that you have but no one has the ability to fulfill your purpose like you. Don't rob the earth of YOU. In today's society we look on the outside in order to find our purpose when our purpose lies inside of YOU. We have this gift in earthen treasures. You're so perfect. You'll never find your true purpose looking on the outside of you. Your purpose is connected to your gift, your purpose is connected to your ability, to make others of your kind. Whatever that gift is connected to, is what you are supposed to leave in this Earth. Gifts are given to be given away.

The number of gifts does not determine the amount of impact. Whether you have one three, five or fourteen gifts it doesn't matter, it's the usage of those gifts that determine your greatness and success. Do not measure or compare your gift to that of someone else. Don't measure or compare the number of gifts you have to someone else because if you take your one gift and do it really well that gift can be just as impactful as someone who has many gifts that they handle with mediocrity. You are unique there is no one like you. You are created to solve a problem in the earth so find that problem and solve it. It's not hard to find, it's down on the inside of you and is connected to the gift. Search your soul and find out the things that you like to do and the things that you do well. According to Webster's definition of a gift is the inherited ability to do something. So, whatever that inherent ability to do, it's your gift. The ability to do something very well, better than others is what's connected to your purpose. So, it's not hard to find. It's a buried treasure is buried down on the inside of you and you only find it by searching on the inside of you. So, search your heart, your mind, your soul, your gift and talent find that purpose and pursue it.

Self-Love Exercise: Take some time and identify what your gifts are? Gift meaning "a notable capacity, talent, or endowment" according to Merriam Webster definition. By identifying your gifts, you will identify you purpose.

1.

2.

3.

4.

5.

Think about the things you have the ability to do and get so much fulfillment that you will do it for free. That is what you are supposed to be doing!!!! List at least 3

1.

2.

3.

Self-Love Journal Exercise:

If finances were not an issue in your life, what would you be doing? Journal about your dream and pursue them.

Day 19 Live Now in the Present

For years I was a victim of what I call Stolen Moments. What I mean by Stolen Moments is you are here in 2020, but you can't embrace it. You can't embrace what is happening right now because of what happened in 2010. It is still holding onto you and is dictating how you move and live in 2020. You are unable to make current decisions because of bad past decisions. We often feel that way because we are not able to push forward. We think we are okay and we go on in life until something happens and then we are faced with the awakening or the disappointment of the past old feelings. Old hurts can be triggered and awakened and it can hold onto you. We are not taught to be in this current moment regardless of what it is. So, if it's happy, sad, hurt, or joyful, embrace where you are right now. Your current moment is an important moment because tomorrow it will be your past. Where you are right now, your current moment is the key to your healing, happiness and success. Not to say that what has happened to you can't help you through what is going on in your life right now but if it is still causing you grief, you have some work to do.

If what you are currently going through is being hindered by the grief of your past there is still some work to do. Love yourself enough to want to be free enough from your past that you can move forward into your future without the past being a hindrance. Think about it this way, you made it through whatever tragedy happen in your life. It didn't kill you and you survived it, so why let the memory of the situation kill. The actual event itself didn't kill you. It's time to take control of your right now. You can't control what happened but you can control what will happen. Embrace you!! Your every moment!! It won't always be good, but every day you are alive it is a chance to change the narrative and to live life differently.

I know you were probably thinking coach that sounds good but is it really something that you can do. My answer is absolutely!! You can live in the right now. Right now, like right now you can feel, live, and embrace you. To get from point A to point B using the GPS it asks to access your current location. That's how you start to live now and not in the past by identifying your current location. You can't tell the GPS where you were or where you want to go without telling it where you are right now. In this journey of self-love, you have to learn to give yourself permission to love you right where you are right now. No longer live your life based on the past but be free to walk in your present. Regardless of the situation and circumstances you can overcome it. You can be free; you just have to take the steps to get to that place. Recognizing where you are and understanding how you got there will help you to not repeat your past mistakes. Acknowledging what you can do differently and making the necessary adjustment is the key to not allowing your past to steal the moments of your present.

Self-Love Exercise: Identify where you are in your life right now if you are not in love with yourself stay out loud, I am not in love with me or I have not been loving me like I should. Think about the areas in your past that always seems to come up and cause havoc in your right now. There may be some people areas or situations you may have to take your power back from; if it has control it has the power.

The Wheel of Life.

Take the time to complete the wheel of life and be honest with yourself about where you currently are. Remember identifying where you currently are is the key to you moving forward in your journey. This will help you identify the areas in your life where you are doing amazing and your areas of opportunity. Rate where you are in this area of life from 1-10. 1 being the lowest and 10 being the highest. This will show you where you need to start to rewrite the narrative of your life.

There is no journal exercise because this exercise takes so soul searching to complete. If it doesn't you didn't do it RIGHT…

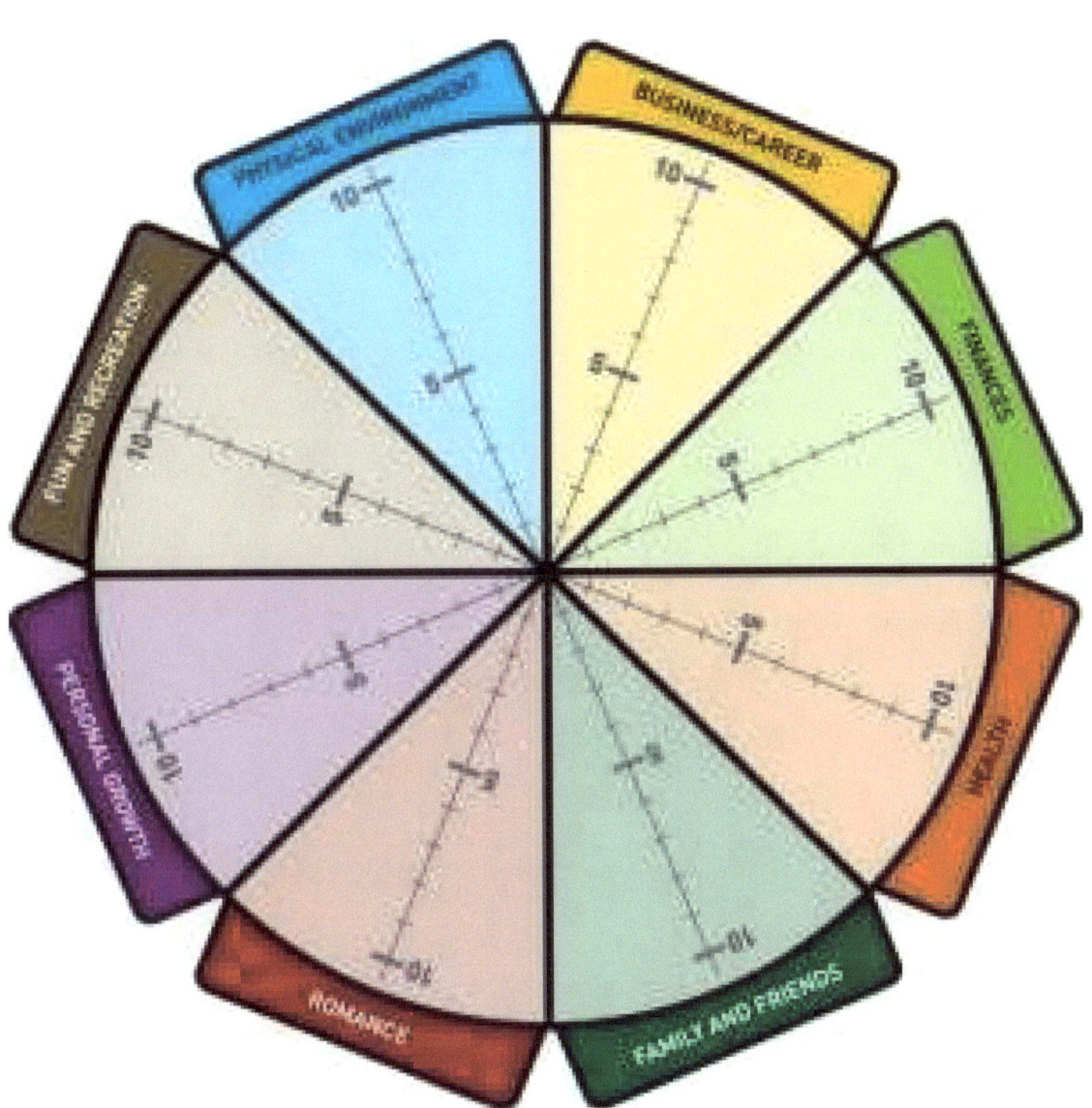

Day 20 No One Compares to You

There is an acronym that has become popular in our time and it is to describe someone who has done something greater than those who has come before them and greater than those who may come after them. People like Michael Jackson, Michael Jordan, Tiger Woods, Barack Obama, Michelle Obama, and Oprah. People of this caliber has been referred to as a G.O.A.T. Meaning they are considered to be the "Greatest of All Times." When I was growing up to refer to someone as a goat was not a term of endearment but now it is one of the highest esteems you can give. The above-named people are all G.O.A.T.S. They are all the greatest of all times. No one else can be compared to them.

There has not been anyone before you or anyone after you who can be compared to you. You are a G.O.A.T. You are the greatest of all time. You might say how can you say that. I can say it with blessed assurance because there will never be another like you. No one before, no one after you. You are the only you. And no one can be a better you than you. You are the best you. There is no comparison to who you are. There is no one who measure up to you. who you are, your success cannot be compared or measured to the success of others. Because there is no one like you. The old cliché' saying "you can't compare apples to oranges." When it comes to comparing you to someone like you or even someone unlike you there is no comparison. Even twins, even though they may share some identical features they are different. So, if twins can't be compared there is absolutely no one on this earth who can compare to you. There is no one who can be measured up to you because only you can be you. You are the greatest you of all the time. Johnathan McReynolds singings a song titled "Comparisons Kill" and they do. Whenever you try to compare your life to someone else's life, you over look how amazingly gifted you are. Comparing your gift to someone else's gift, may cause you to feel like you are insignificant. What you view as success to someone else may be a failure to them and you overlook your success. Although identical twins share some features and DNA, they are different so if a twin can't be compared there is absolutely no one on this earth who can be compared to you. I say to you that you are the greatest you of all time. No one can do you like you. No one can be like you. So, embrace you and be confident in you knowing that when you walk in the building no one can do you like you do.

One of my favorite parts of the song Comparison Kills says "The grass was fine until it looks greener on the other side. Now you believing that you fell behind. Why try to match what should be one of a kind. You're one of a kind" I love this part of the song because we are often times in a good space until we start to look and compare ourselves to the liking of someone else. You are great just as you. Be okay in the skin you're in because no one can compare to you.

Self-Love Exercise: For the next 3 days look yourself in the eyes and tell yourself **"THERE IS NO ONE AS GREAT AS YOU"**

Self-Love Journal: Every day after telling yourself "THERE IS NO ONE AS GREAT AS YOU" Journal how it made you feel. You should tell yourself this daily. This is just the start of you knowing that you are great.

Day 21 Make Time for You

We take time for so many things, so many people, and so much stuff. We plan, we set aside and we coordinate time to spend with others but the one of the things that gets neglected is spending time with is yourself. We find ourselves burned out and frustrated and ready to give up because we do not take time for ourselves, time to reset, recharge, and unwind. So, we continue to go day after day without taking time to gather our thoughts and just be in a quiet moment with ourselves. We may think that with all we do there is no time for us to take a day to ourselves and I agree but you have to schedule time in your day for you. To make time for yourself just like you plan time that you spend with other people. You have to plan time to spend with yourself, you will discover that there is a lot about you that you are unaware of because you have never taken the time to get to know you.

In this journey of discovery of self-love, in order for you to learn to love you, you have to take time to discover who you are and get to know yourself. Whenever we are courting or dating someone, we take time to find out what they like and their dislikes, their beliefs and what they like to do. Because we want to know them for who they are but I want to pose this question to you. Who are you? Have you taken the time to find out Who You Are? Have you taken to the time to find out what you have down on the inside of you? Most of us have not, but in order for you to learn to love you and identify more ways to connect to you and love more on you that requires you spending time with yourself.

I remember a time in my life when I did not like the person I had become and did not want to spend time with that person because of the things I allowed to take place in my life. Because of the abuse I allowed to take place in my life. I discovered I was no longer the victim of my hurt but a participant. I didn't like looking at myself in the mirror because I did not know who I was anymore. So, I had to peel back the hurt, the dysfunction, the abuse and the disappointment that I had in me in order to love me. But once I accepted the fact that I had taken part in allowing my abuser to abuse me, I could then start to do the work. I realized I helped him hurt me.

Because I took ownership in the place I was in my life and my discovery of learning to love myself. I started spending more time with me and less time with others. Myles Monroe has the series names "The Five Keys to Success" and the first key to success is learning "who am I?" I want to pose this question to you again Who are you?

Before you answer the question don't think about who you are connected to, don't think about the fact that you are parent or wife, a partner, the company you work for, your religious affiliation, and don't think about being a child because none of those things are who you are. So, asked that question To yourself "who am I?" Learning to love yourself will begin with you learning who you are and spending time with you.

I started with simply taking 7 minutes in the morning to myself. Before my feet hit the floor, I take time for me. I use this time to meditate pray and center myself. This helps me to focus better on my day and it gets me grounded. I get up at 5:30am. I have a 5:30am alarm and then I have a 5:37am alarm. This is me being intentional about the time I spend with me. Making myself a priority

It doesn't seem like a lot of time but it is not about the quantity but the quality. Research states how you spend the first 20 minutes of your day will determine the outcome of your day. It will determine how successful your day will be.

Ever since I started taking this time for myself, I am more focused and less stressed. Learn to be intentional about spending time with you.

Self-Love Exercise: Tomorrow schedule at least 7 minutes to yourself. Nothing is important but the taking time. The location, the time, what will be done doesn't matter just be intentional and schedule the time. Commit yourself to this time for 21 days. Be protective over this time and be vigilant about keeping this time. In this journey to Self-Love being committed to you will be essential to you remaining in a good place with YOU.

Self-Love Journal: Answer the question Who Are You?

Self-Love Journal

Self-Love Journal

Self-Love Journal

Self-Love Journal

Self-Love Journal

Self-Love Journal

Self-Love Journal

Self-Love Journal

Self-Love Journal

Self-Love Journal

Self-Love Journal

Self-Love Journal

Self-Love Journal

Self-Love Journal

Self-Love Journal

Self-Love Journal

Self-Love Journal

Self-Love Journal

Self-Love Journal

Self-Love Journal

Self-Love Journal

Self-Love Journal

Self-Love Journal

Self-Love Journal

Self-Love Journal

THE LIFE NAVIGATOR

About Coach Mechelle

Mechelle D. Canady, a seasoned Event Planner, Certified Master Life Coach, Author, Trainer and Innovator who is driven by an unwavering entrepreneurial spirit. Her dedication to helping people become their best versions has also earned her the reputation as "The Life Navigator."

SPEAKER TOPICS
The 3'A to Change
Don't Die with Purpose
Knowing Your Worth at Work
Conflict Management
How to Be A World Changer

Impact, Impart, Empower

Published Books
Frozen: 3 A's My Journey to True Forgiveness
Overcoming Toxic Relationships
21 Day Journey to Self-Love Workbook
Change Your Posture Affirmation Journal

Specializing in
Curriculm Development
Customized Workshops
Team Building Activity
Interactive Workshops
Conference Hosting and more

CERTIFICATIONS
Certifed Master Life Coach
Certified Train the Trainer
Executive Trainer

Contact Coach Mechelle Canady
904-609-4134
coachmechellecanady@gmail.com
Follow her on Facebook, Instagram & Twitter
@coachmechellecanady

www.ingramcontent.com/pod-product-compliance
Lightning Source LLC
Chambersburg PA
CBHW041957150426
43193CB00003B/41